SPARKY'S STEM GUIDE TO...
MOTORBIKES

BY KIRSTY HOLMES

BookLife PUBLISHING

©2019
BookLife Publishing Ltd.
King's Lynn
Norfolk PE30 4LS

All rights reserved.
Printed in Malaysia.

A catalogue record for this book is available from the British Library.

ISBN: 978-1-78637-804-0

Written by:
Kirsty Holmes

Edited by:
Emilie Dufresne

Designed by:
Danielle Rippengill

All facts, statistics, web addresses and URLs in this book were verified as valid and accurate at time of writing. No responsibility for any changes to external websites or references can be accepted by either the author or publisher.

Original idea by Harrison Holmes.

IMAGE CREDITS

All images are courtesy of Shutterstock.com, unless otherwise specified. With thanks to Getty Images, Thinkstock Photo and iStockphoto. Cover – NotionPic, A–R–T, logika600, BiterBig, Marharyta Pavliuk, SugarDesign. Sparky – NotionPic, Marharyta Pavliuk. Peggy – NotionPic. Grid – BiterBig. Construction School – Mascha Tace. 2 – . 5 – Mascha Tace. 6 – Ivengo. 7 – MuchMania. 8 – Ivengo. 10 – Flat vectors. 11 – Dzianis_Rakhuba. 12 – KittyVector. 12 & 13 – Ivengo, MuchMania. 13 – Igogosha. 16 – Alex Leo, Shirstok. 17 – Ivengo. 18 & 19 – MuchMania, KittyVector. 20 – Mascha Tace. 21 – ArtMalivanov, DRogatnev. 22 – Alexandr III, VectorsMarket, Meth Mehr. 23 – Mascha Tace, Alexandr Kahovski.

CONTENTS

PAGE 4 — Welcome to Driving School!

PAGE 6 — Lesson 1: What Is a Motorbike?

PAGE 8 — Lesson 2: Parts of a Motorbike

PAGE 10 — Lesson 3: Riding a Motorbike

PAGE 12 — Lesson 4: Types of Motorbike

PAGE 14 — Lesson 5: Steering!

PAGE 16 — Lesson 6: Wheelies!

PAGE 18 — Lesson 7: Mega Motorbike

PAGE 20 — Driving Test

PAGE 22 — Bonus Lesson: Ramp to Ramp

PAGE 24 — Glossary and Index

Words that look like this can be found in the glossary on page 24.

WELCOME TO DRIVING SCHOOL!

VROOM! I'm Jeremy Sparkplug, world-famous motorbike racer. You can call me Sparky. You must be the new recruits. Welcome to the Horses for Courses School of Motoring!

Here you will be learning about some of the fastest – and coolest – **vehicles** on two wheels: motorbikes! Pay attention, because if you pass your driving test, you'll earn your Golden Horseshoe.

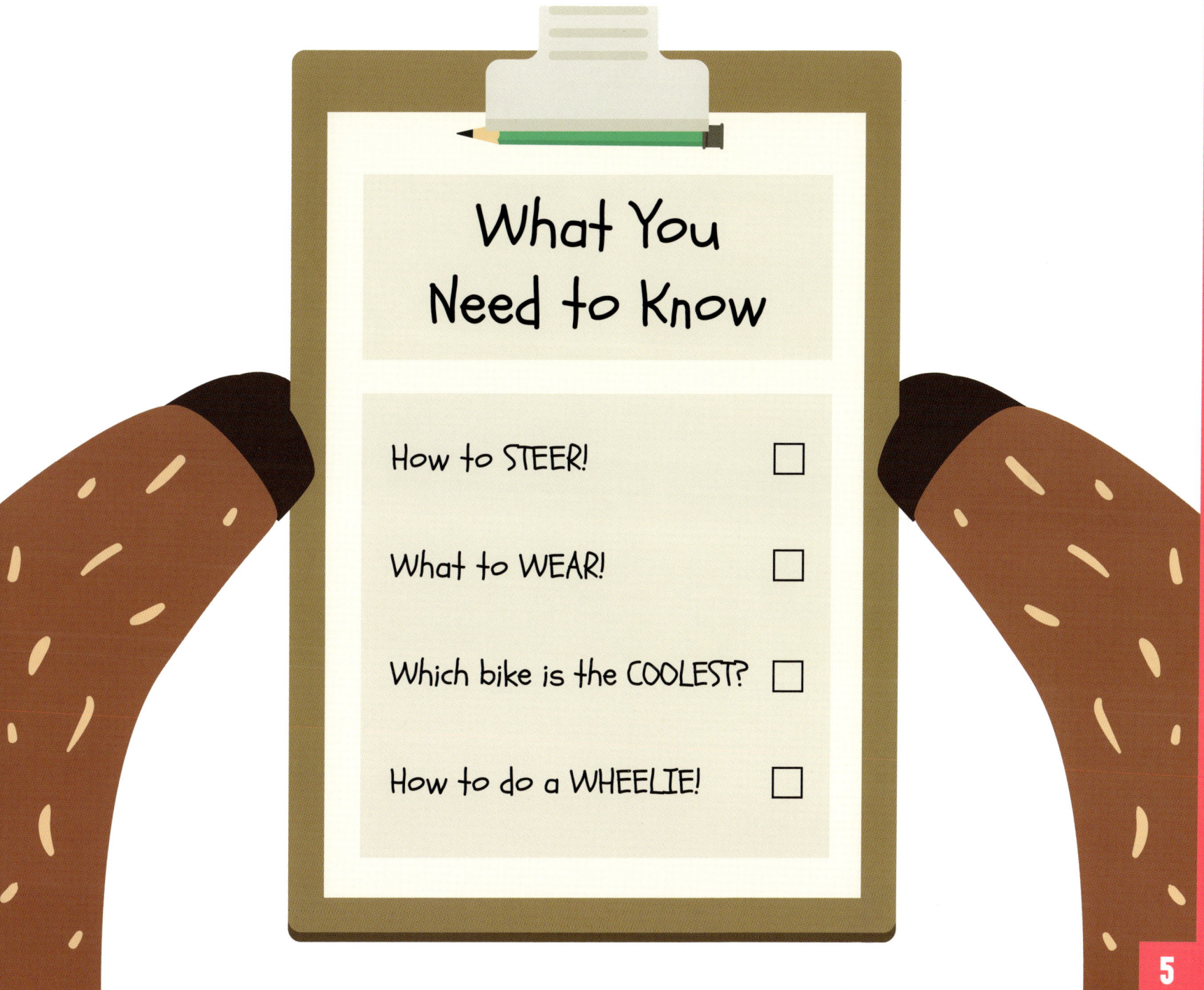

What You Need to Know

How to STEER! ☐

What to WEAR! ☐

Which bike is the COOLEST? ☐

How to do a WHEELIE! ☐

Lesson 1: What is a Motorbike?

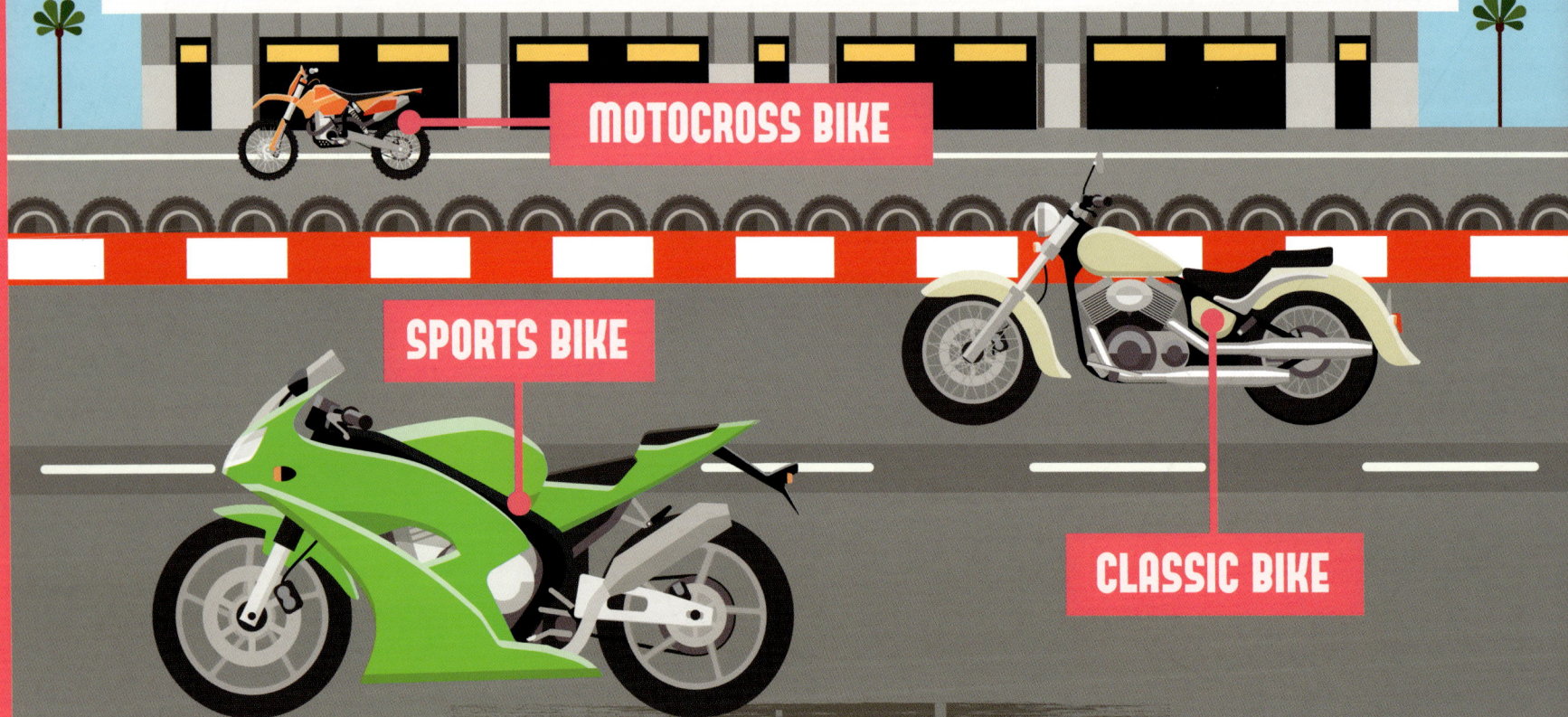

MOTOCROSS BIKE

SPORTS BIKE

CLASSIC BIKE

A motorbike is a vehicle that usually has two wheels, a seat for the driver (and sometimes a passenger), and an engine. Motorbikes are mostly for getting one or two people from one place to another.

Lesson 2: Parts of a Motorbike

Suspension
This helps the bike bounce on the road, making it more comfortable for the rider.

Front Fork
This holds the front wheel in place, and allows the rider to steer.

Engine
The engine provides the power for the motorbike.

Brakes
Brakes stop the motorbike.

Wheels
Wheels are made of metal, and have tyres that are usually made of **rubber**.

In a car, you are protected from the weather and accidents by the roof and doors. On a motorbike, your clothing has to do the job of protecting you instead. This special clothing is often called 'gear'.

LEATHERS — Protect the body

HELMET — Protects the head

VISOR — Protects the face

KNEE PADS — Protect the knees

Lesson 3: Riding a Motorbike

Let's take a look at the **dashboard** to see how to steer and control a motorbike.

CLUTCH LEVER
This is for selecting and changing **gear**.

SPEEDOMETER
This tells the rider how fast they are going.

TACHOMETER
This helps the rider know when to change gear.

WING MIRRORS
The rider uses these to see behind them.

BRAKE LEVER
This is for slowing down and stopping.

LIGHT SWITCH
This turns the lights on and off.

HANDLEBARS
These are for steering the bike.

THROTTLE
Twisting this handgrip controls the speed of the motorbike.

Some motorbikes have only one seat, but others have a second seat for passengers. This special second seat is called the pillion seat. Passengers on a bike are 'riding pillion'.

Lesson 4: Types of Motorbike

There are lots of different types of motorbike. Let's look at some of the more popular ones.

Scooters

Scooters have a platform for the rider's feet.

Touring Bikes

These are sturdy and comfortable for riding long distances.

Sports Bikes

These bikes are built for speed and power. They are **designed** for roads and racing tracks.

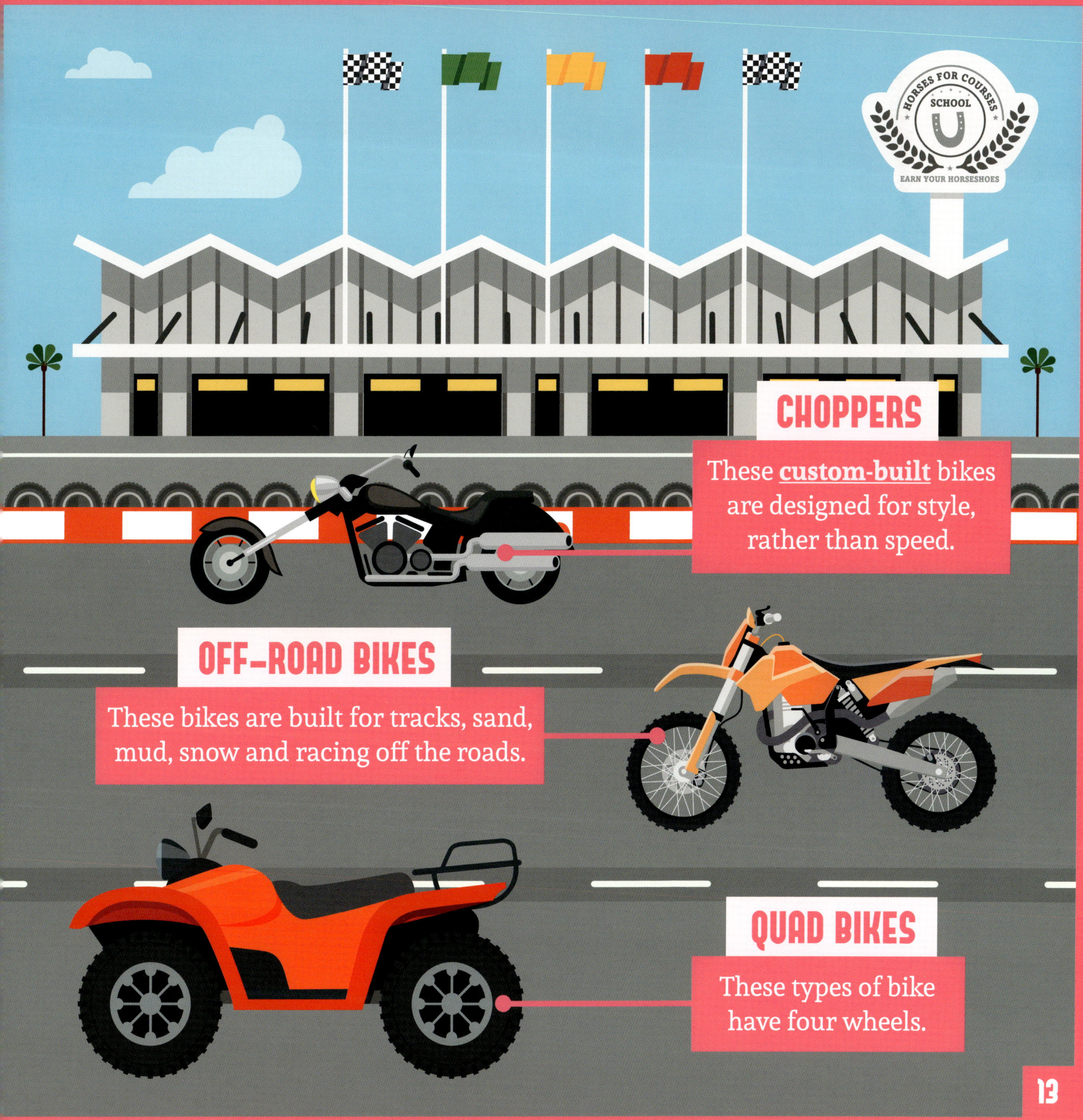

CHOPPERS

These **custom-built** bikes are designed for style, rather than speed.

OFF-ROAD BIKES

These bikes are built for tracks, sand, mud, snow and racing off the roads.

QUAD BIKES

These types of bike have four wheels.

LESSON 5:
STEERING!

You might think steering a motorbike is just like steering your bike in the park. However, there is a little more to it than that...

STEER IN THE DIRECTION YOU WANT TO GO...

...AND THE BIKE WILL TURN WITHOUT LEANING.

SLOW SPEEDS

To turn right at slow speeds, you push the left handlebar forwards and pull the right one towards you.

FAST SPEEDS

At fast speeds, instead of pushing the left handlebar, you slightly push the right one. The bike leans the opposite way, and <u>arcs</u> around the turn. This is called countersteering.

STEER
Steer in the opposite direction, just for a moment...

TURN
...and the bike will lean into the turn.

LESSON 6:
WHEELIES!

OK, class. While Sparky is distracted polishing his bike, I'm going to teach you something really, really cool. This is how to do a wheelie...

STEP ONE
Start at 10–20 kilometres per hour.

STEP TWO
Hit the throttle and speed up – hard!

STEP THREE
Lean back and pull the front wheel up... Wheelie!

It takes a lot of practice to do the perfect wheelie – so when you're older, and you've passed all your tests, I'll give you another lesson!

Lesson 7: Mega Motorbike

The Regio Design XXL Chopper

Fabio Reggiani's custom-built chopper is one of the biggest motorbikes in the world. It is over five metres tall, almost ten metres long, and weighs around 4,000 kilograms!

DRIVING TEST

Right, bikers. It's time to earn your Golden Horseshoe. Safely make your way to the test centre... I said safely! Who taught you to do a wheelie like that... and can they teach me?

Questions

1. What does the suspension do?

2. What does a visor protect?

3. What is 'riding pillion'?

4. When countersteering, which handlebar should you push first if you want to go right?

5. How tall is the Regio Design XXL Chopper?

Did you get them all right?

Of course you did – here is your Golden Horseshoe. You are now officially in the Cool Bikers Club, just like Peggy and me!

Answers: 1. Makes it bouncy and comfortable. 2. Your face. 3. Riding as a passenger. 4. Push the right handlebar to go right. 5. Over five meters!

BONUS LESSON:
RAMP TO RAMP

Motorbikes are great for getting about, having fun on the track, and looking cool. But in our expert hooves, they are also great for MAD, CRAZY STUNTS!

STEP ONE
Get some buses...

STEP TWO
Ramp it up...

STEP THREE
Start your engines...

GLOSSARY

ARCS — travels on a curved line or path

CUSTOM-BUILT — built specially for one person, exactly how they want it

DASHBOARD — the area facing the driver of a vehicle, which contains the controls for driving

DESIGNED — when something is specially made for a specific purpose

GEAR — a part of a machine that moves other parts

RUBBER — a bouncy material made from tropical plants

VEHICLES — machines used for carrying or transporting things or people

INDEX

CHOPPERS 7, 13, 18, 20

OFF-ROAD BIKES 13

QUAD BIKES 13

RACING 12–13

RIDERS 8, 10, 12

SCOOTERS 7, 12

SPORTS BIKES 6, 12

STEERING 5, 8, 10, 14–15, 20

TOURING BIKES 7, 12

TYRES 8, 19

WHEELIES 5, 7, 16–17, 20

WHEELS 5–6, 8, 13, 16

24